MW00388334

No
Barking
at the table
Cookbook

No
Barking
at the table
Cookbook

More Recipes Your Dog Will Beg For

Written by
Wendy Nan Rees

Illustrations by
Hillary Huber Wilson

HOWELL BOOK HOUSE
NEW YORK

Copyright © 1996 by Wendy Nan Rees

All rights reserved. No part of this book may be reproduced or transmitted in any form or by any means, electronic or mechanical, including photocopying, recording, or by any information storage and retrieval system, without permission in writing from the Publisher.

Howell Book House
A Simon & Schuster Macmillan Company
1633 Broadway
New York, NY 10019

MACMILLAN is a registered trademark of Macmillan, Inc.

Library of Congress Cataloging-in-Publication Data
Rees, Wendy N.
        No barking at the table: more recipes your dog will beg for / Wendy
Nan Rees : drawings by Hillary Huber Wilson.
                p. cm.
        Includes index.
        ISBN 0-87605-694-X (alk. paper)
        1. Dogs—Food—Recipes. I. Title.
SF427.4.R44 1996   96-12819
636.7'0855—dc20   CIP
Manufactured in the United States of America
10 9 8 7 6 5 4 3 2 1

Book design by George J. McKeon

I dedicate this book to my mom and dad, Ambassador Alan and Melinda Blinken, for their love and support. They encouraged me to continue my education despite my dyslexia. Their belief that I am a special person has enabled me to do anything I set my heart on, and helped me to create and achieve my goals.

Thank you with all my love,
Wendy

For Rudy and Isabel Wilson.

With love,
Mommy

CONTENTS

Contents

ABOUT THE AUTHOR

. . . .

Since she was two years old, Wendy Nan Rees has loved animals. Her first pets were an English Setter named Digby and a pony named Ricky, and over the years she's grown attached to many more dogs, cats, horses—you name it. Now her love of animals and her concern for their health and well-being have led Wendy to become an entrepreneur and author. She is the creator of Lip Smackers, a company dedicated to providing healthy, all-natural treats for pets. She has also written a book on how and why people name their pets called *The Name Game*. Wendy lives in Los Angeles with her husband Tom and her two best friends, Stella Bella and Governor.

About the Illustrator

Hillary Huber Wilson is a freelance artist who lives in Los Angeles with her family and her dog, Racine. Having spent the better part of her artistic career in painting, ceramics and graphic design, she is now turning her attention to illustration.

ACKNOWLEDGMENTS

It is not possible to give thanks to all those responsible for helping me achieve one of my dreams. It surely never would have happened without the help and support of my husband, Tom, whose patience is everlasting.

Many thanks to my editors, Felice Primeau and Ariel Cannon—your support is so appreciated. My thanks to Bethann Wetzel. We've been through a lot together, and I'm sure there were times when my sanity was in serious doubt. Thanks to Paula Turner for her love and support, and Liza Reisenbach and her dog Louie for taste-testing so many recipes.

My thanks to all of you who have given me your help, love, and support: Carol Ann Blinken Emquies, Ruth & Howard W. Koch, Steve LuKanic (what a special friend), and Dot Stovall (you always know how to capture the moment).

Special thanks goes to Lewis Turner. He has bred new life to my dreams and goals. I tell him to always keep the magic coming.

Thanks also to the contributors, Eliane Fahim, Paula Turner and Bethann Wetzel, for their delicious recipes. You will also find a number of recipes subtitled "From Kelly Ann's Kitchen." My dear friend, Kelly Ann McNabb, has taught me a lot about cooking, and it gives me great pleasure to include

Acknowledgments

each of the recipes she provided. This is the first of many projects we will work on together. Thank you Kelly.

As you can see, my friends and family have all lent their support to this book. Thank you.

PREFACE

One of the first things I wanted to have after graduating from college was a dog, not just an ordinary dog, but a Chinese Shar-Pei. After a great deal of searching I found the perfect one—Webster. When I got him home, he looked like one big ball of wrinkles and, except for his head, he eventually grew into them.

When Webster was just a few months old, I began noticing digestive and skin problems. Our veterinarian took tests and diagnosed him with a soy allergy. I thought it would be easy enough to find a food that would agree with him and meet my high standards for nutritional value. I did discover a kibble that he enjoyed, but I ran into some problems finding biscuits for treats.

Most of the biscuits were made up of ingredients that either I didn't want Webster to eat or he simply didn't like. The quest had begun to find the right biscuit. After many trials and tribulations, I decided to test my talents in the kitchen and create a biscuit myself. In this way, I'd have control of the ingredients and besides . . . how difficult could it be to bake a dog biscuit? I was surprised to find that it was actually quite complicated. I went through batch after batch after batch. They would fall apart, or look like oatmeal, or Webster would turn up his bulbous nose and politely walk away.

. . . .

It took almost a year before finding the right combination of ingredients. I noticed that one particular batch had a mouth-watering aroma. Before the biscuits hardened, I tasted them and found they were particularly good. After they had cooled, I called Webster over for the ultimate test. Not only did he eat one, he wanted another. This recipe had definite possibilities.

Before long, people dropped by the kitchen to find out what the delicious smell was. They too participated in the "taste test." The general response was that the biscuits were a bit bland, but not bad. When I divulged that these were made for Webster, some laughed and others had "interesting" expressions.

During the holiday season I became inundated with requests from friends and family to make up orders. As demand increased, I gave more and more thought to enhancing what was, by then, a part-time job. I finally decided to put all of my efforts into producing and merchandising Webster's cookies, and after discussing the cookies with friends and family, the name "Lip Smackers" was born.

Originally we packed the cookies in Chinese "to go" cartons with a drawing of Webster on the front. We spent hours baking biscuits, labeling cartons, hand packing and delivering them to stores. This was only the beginning.

The carton soon changed to a bag, and the number of stores carrying Lip Smackers grew. As our popularity grew, we created a new, eye-catching box design.

Since cooking for both the two- and four-legged members of my family was one of my greatest pleasures, I kept an extensive file of my favorite recipes. One day it struck me that there were others who would enjoy a cookbook on canine cuisine. I began the process of writing, re-writing, cooking, tasting and testing. Once again, I found myself involved in a project that was much more exciting than I had imagined. I have created easy-to-prepare recipes that will be fun for the whole family. Enjoy!

—Wendy Nan Rees

INTRODUCTION

. . . .

The purpose of this book is to provide suggestions to "liven" up your dog's diet. I have prepared all the recipes included here and fed them to Webster and other dogs who genuinely enjoyed them. *These recipes are simply a supplement to your dog's diet and are not designed to replace it.*

If you are concerned or curious about any of the ingredients or preparations, please seek the advice of your veterinarian. Each dog's needs and reactions are different. In fact, it was Webster's special requirements that led to the creation of Lip Smackers dog biscuits.

One of the objectives of this book is to encourage parents to bring their children into the kitchen. Using the family dog as the incentive might act as a springboard for other activities—like helping out with dinner. I have had especially good responses from parents with handicapped children. Due to the ease of preparation of most of the recipes, those with physical and/or mental handicaps can participate. Activities like these help to build confidence and learning skills, and children will be proud of helping to make something special for their pet.

Although our awareness in the area of human nutrition has improved dramatically, there has not been enough attention paid to our pets' foods. We hope to help you become more conscious of their nutritional needs by talking to your veterinarian and reading about what you are feeding your pet. Preservatives, salt and poor-quality ingredients have the same impact on pets as they do on humans.

So turn to the section that intrigues you, get the kids (both two- and four-legged) and start cooking!

BEFORE YOU BEGIN

. . . .

A lot of recipes in this book call for boiled chicken livers or boiled chicken pieces. To do this, in a large saucepan or small stockpot full of cold water (approximately 5 cups of cold water to every pound of meat) add 1 or 2 onions and a bay leaf for flavor. The onions can later be ground up with the chicken livers, but always remove the bay leaf. Bring chicken pieces or livers to a boil and simmer for 25 to 30 minutes uncovered. Then drain. They can be served plain or used in other recipes. *Always* wait for food to cool before serving.

I have specifically selected ingredients that are fresh, wholesome and readily available. Also, chopped fresh parsley not only adds flavor but also chlorophyll which helps freshen breath. You can purchase brewer's yeast at a health food store. Feel free to add this to any recipe (as in the cookie recipes) as many people think it helps to control fleas and aids in digestion. Most of my recipes call for beef or chicken stock (or broth). I like the low-salt version which can be purchased in a can from the supermarket. If you wish to make your own stock, a recipe can be found on page 84.

A Word from Webster and Max

All the recipes in this wonderful book were made just for me, Webster. Well, okay, *mostly* for me.

My first memories of Wendy are from my pup days in Atlanta, Georgia. I was one mass of wrinkles and got lots of strange looks, but Wendy kept telling me people stared because I was special. We appeared in many dog shows and I was so nervous that I usually ended up with an upset stomach. It wasn't long before we found out I had a problem called colitis.

Wendy began experimenting with all sorts of foods to see how my stomach would react. I remember pots and pans flying around the kitchen and a lot of cooking going on! It was cookie heaven. Some tasted good, some were fair and, to be honest, some were so bad I had to escape to the backyard. But one particular afternoon (how could I forget?), she took the best-smelling biscuits ever out of the oven. Wendy named them "Webster's Cookies." Now they're called Lip Smackers—different name, but still my recipe!

Around this time, Max moved next door and soon we became the best of friends. (Max's mom is pretty cool, too—she gives a mean water bowl!) Max is much more outgoing than me and thrives on attention. His ultimate fantasy is to be on the cover of *Dog World*; I much prefer the quiet life.

It seemed like there were always friends and relatives visiting us, and Wendy would constantly be whipping up a creation or two. Occasionally, she had help: Aunt Beth would cook up a pretty terrific rice dish along with some very outrageous desserts, and Kelly spoiled us with her delicious treats. For years, we were "hounding" Wendy to print up some of her favorite recipes. It was partly selfish (what if she forgets them?), but we also wanted to share the tasty recipes so others could enjoy them, too.

As Wendy and her friends cooked madly, Hillary, with pencil and pad constantly in hand, kept us laughing with her clever and humorous sketches. I think Wendy must have shown her our family album!

Well, I promised Max he could share a few words with you. Watch out—he can talk forever!

Well, finally I get to tell you my side of the story. Oh, oh. . . . Sniff, Sniff, Sniff. . . . Smells like lunch is being served. Sorry, can't talk now. . . . Gotta eat!

—WEBSTER & MAX

Snicks and Snacks from Webster and Max

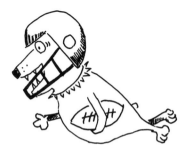

The Super Bowl Party

In January everyone becomes obsessed with football (at least from my point of view, they're obsessed). As the playoffs draw to a close and the Super Bowl is upon us, bets are placed and invitations ring out "Super Bowl party at Wendy's place!"

Making snacks for your pet doesn't have to be long and involved. This section is simplicity at its best, a key to a last-minute doggie delight. Fix these sporty specialties when you want to score big time!

Cheese Toast Points

Serves 6

3 tablespoons grated Parmesan cheese

1 teaspoon paprika

6 slices brown cocktail bread, cut in triangles

Sprinkle cheese and paprika on bread. Toast under broiler until lightly brown.

Meatball Cocktail

Serves 6

1   pound ground beef

1/2 cup cooked brown rice

1   small onion, chopped

1   tablespoon ketchup

1   egg, beaten

2   tablespoons chopped fresh parsley

Preheat oven to 350 degrees.

Mix all ingredients together. Form meat into small balls. Bake in a 9 x 12" baking dish for 45 to 55 minutes. Cool and serve.

Quiche Lorraine for the Bacon & Egg Lover

Without the pastry pie shell.

Serves 6

6 slices low-salt bacon, cut in half

4 eggs

1 tablespoon all-purpose flour

2 cups light cream

pinch of nutmeg

1 1/2 tablespoons melted butter

12 thin slices Swiss cheese, cut in strips

Preheat oven to 375 degrees.

Cook bacon and set aside. Beat eggs and add flour, nutmeg and cream. Stir in melted butter. Place bacon and cheese in layers in a glass pie pan. Pour egg mixture over and bake for 45 minutes to 1 hour. Serve cool.

Liver Drops

Serves 6

5 cups water

1 chicken bouillon cube

1 small onion, chopped

1 pound chicken livers

1 cup seasoned bread crumbs mixed with two tablespoons wheat germ

Combine water and bouillon cube in a large saucepan and bring to a boil. Add onion and liver; boil until tender. Drain. Take liver and onion and place in blender or food processor. Blend until mixture is stiff with small chunks; form into small balls. Roll meatballs in bread-crumb mixture. Place on a lightly greased cookie sheet and bake until golden brown. Let liver drops cool and serve. This may be frozen in single-serving portions.

FIDO

Liver Drops are great for enticing your performer at a dog show, or just as little tongue pleasers.

Prosciutto with Cheese Sticks

Serves 6

  6 slices boiled ham

1/2 block cheddar cheese

Slice cheese into sticks and place one in center of each slice of ham. Roll. Serve immediately.

FIDO

Prosciutto is far too expensive. We use boiled ham and Webster and Max love it—but they still like to call it prosciutto.

Eggs for the Devil on a Diet

Serves 6

     6 hard-boiled eggs, halved. Set aside the yolks

1 1/4 cups nonfat cottage cheese

   1/2 teaspoon onion powder

   1/2 teaspoon garlic powder

In a blender or food processor mix egg yolks, cottage cheese, onion and garlic powders. Blend well. Pipe (spoon) into the egg halves.

You may garnish egg halves with a sprinkle of paprika.

7

Tuna Pâté

When plain tuna fish just won't do.

Serves 4

Many are surprised to find that their pooch likes fish. Cats have not cornered the market after all.

1 12-ounce can of tuna

1 tablespoon olive oil

2 teaspoons grated onion

4 tablespoons cottage cheese

1 teaspoon lemon juice

Blend tuna, olive oil, onion and cottage cheese in a blender or food processor. Add lemon juice. Mold and chill until ready to serve.

FIDO

Dark tuna is preferred in our house as it is richer and more flavorful. What's most important is that Webster and Max love it.

Puppy Love

St. Valentine's Day

Wouldn't it be nice to spend all winter by a fire staring into our loved one's eyes, eating foods to warm our hearts?

Stews are easy, healthy meals as they contain various, complimentary food groups. Max especially enjoys the carrots. I don't think this vegetable has improved his eyesight, although he never has a problem finding his plate.

FROM ELAINE'S KITCHEN

Rice for the True Rice Lover

Serves 4

- 1 small bunch of vermicelli (thin spaghetti)
- 1 tablespoon butter
- 1 cup long grain white rice
- 1 1/2 cups water

Break vermicelli into small pieces and sauté with butter in a saucepan until slightly brown. Add rice, brown slightly, then add water. Bring to a boil. Cover and simmer for 20 minutes. Serve at room temperature.

FIDO

This is Webster's favorite. He likes to add a dollop of plain yogurt!

A Stew to Warm Any Heart

Serves 6

1 pound stewing beef, cubed

20 small button onions, peeled

5 carrots, chunked

2 1/2 cups boiling water mixed with 2 beef bouillon cubes

1 cup canned corn

1 bay leaf

2 cloves garlic, chopped

1 tablespoon yellow cornmeal mixed with 2 table-spoons cold water

Preheat oven to 325 degrees.

Mix the first seven ingredients. Bake in a Dutch oven for 2 hours. Add cornmeal mixture and mix well. Return to oven for another 30 minutes. Remove the bay leaf before serving.

For the dog on a low-salt diet, you may substitute low-salt beef broth for beef bouillon cubes: 1 cup water with 1 1/2 cups beef broth.

This can be frozen in single-serving portions.

FIDO

Always remember to remove the bay leaf before serving.

Chicken Stew

Serves 6

 1 pound deboned chicken, cubed (light or dark meat)

10 small button onions, peeled

 5 carrots, chunked

 1 cup peas (frozen can be used)

2 1/2 cups boiling water mixed with 2 chicken bouillon cubes

 1 bay leaf

 1 tablespoon yellow cornmeal mixed with 2 tablespoons cold water

Preheat oven to 325 degrees.

Mix the first six ingredients. Bake in a Dutch oven for 1 hour. Add cornmeal mixture and mix well. Return to oven for another 30 minutes. Remove the bay leaf before serving.

For the dog on a low-salt diet, you may substitute low-salt chicken broth for beef bouillon cubes: 1 cup water with 1 1/2 cups low-salt chicken broth.

This can be frozen in single-serving portions.

Try serving this at room temperature over kibble.

13

Basic Burger for Two

Serves 2

1 pound ground beef

1 tablespoon onion powder

1 tablespoon chopped fresh parsley

2 tablespoons A.1 Sauce

In a large bowl mix all ingredients together. Form meat mixture into two hamburger patties and grill until done.

FIDO

A Dutch oven is a large pot with a tight-fitting lid, made of cast iron or another strong material. You can cook with it on top of the stove, or bake with it in the oven.

Green
and Lean

St. Patty's Day

On St. Patrick's Day I woke to find a world gone green. Before me there lay a breakfast of Irish delight. Green . . . green . . . green eggs, green milk, green oatmeal. If Dr. Seuss could do it, then why not Maureen McNulty Wetzel? We loved it so that, to this day, we still celebrate St. Patty's Day with green food!

Maureen's Green Eggs

Serves 2

2   eggs

2   drops green food coloring (adjust to desired color)

1/4   cup cooked diced ham

1   teaspoon butter or margarine

Beat eggs, add green food coloring and ham. Heat skillet with butter or margarine. Pour in egg mixture and cook slowly over medium heat until done.

FROM KELLY ANN'S KITCHEN

Half-Baked Broccoli

Serves 4

1 large bunch of broccoli, cut into bite-size pieces

1/2 cup fresh bread crumbs

2 cloves garlic, crushed

1 cup wheat germ

1/2 cup extra-light olive oil

2 hard-boiled eggs

1/2 cup Swiss cheese, grated

Preheat oven to 325 degrees.

Steam broccoli for 5 to 7 minutes. Sauté bread crumbs, garlic and wheat germ in olive oil until tender and golden brown (3 to 4 minutes). Alternately layer casserole dish with broccoli and bread-crumb mixture. Repeat until both mixtures are used up. Top casserole with sliced hard-boiled eggs and Swiss cheese. Bake for 25 minutes.

FROM KELLY ANN'S KITCHEN

Green, Mean Zucchini Casserole

Serves 6

4 cups grated zucchini (set in a colander with
1/2 tablespoon salt over it to drain)

1/2 cup grated Swiss cheese

1 cup all-purpose flour

2 teaspoons fast-acting baking powder

2 eggs, beaten

1 cup half-and-half

   salt and pepper to taste

Preheat oven to 325 degrees.

Mix all ingredients together and put into a buttered baking dish. Bake for 35 to 45 minutes until golden brown.

A Sunday Munch

Easter Brunch

Ask any pup what they do on Easter. Most will say, "Hunt for the Easter eggs!" Max and Webster always run through my garden (oh no!) competing for the most eggs. When all is said and done, baskets are full, the feast enjoyed and the soil has been turned for spring flowers.

Health Jacks

PANCAKES FOR EASTER BRUNCH

Serves 4

3/4 cup rolled oats

3/4 cup lowfat milk

1/2 teaspoon baking soda

1/4 cup whole-wheat flour

  1 egg, beaten

1/2 teaspoon vanilla

In a blender or food processor chop oats. In a large bowl, mix oats and milk. Put aside for 5 minutes. Add baking soda, flour, egg and vanilla and mix. Spoon small amounts into a hot buttered skillet. Serve with a dollop of cottage cheese.

FIDO

These flapjacks don't weigh you down. I've made them for the family (two- and four-legged). Skip the butter and syrup for the four-legged.

So Why Do They Call Them "Scotch Eggs"?

Serves 6

2 pounds ground beef (may substitute half the ground beef with ground pork)

1 tablespoon fresh parsley

2 tablespoons finely grated Parmesan cheese

1/2 cup bread crumbs

2 eggs, beaten lightly

6 hard-boiled eggs

3 tablespoons olive oil

Preheat oven to 325 degrees.

Mix ground beef, parsley, cheese, bread crumbs and 2 eggs until blended. Mold ground-beef mixture around shelled hard-boiled eggs. Brown in olive oil, then transfer to baking dish. Bake for 20 to 25 minutes or until done.

Nuthin' but Mutton (and Veggie) Stew

Serves 6

2	tablespoons olive oil
1 1/2	pounds cubed lamb shoulder
1	large onion, chopped
2	cloves garlic, minced
1/2	cup low-salt tomato sauce
1/2	cup chopped carrots
1/2	cup cubed zucchini
2	cups water
1/2	cup peas (frozen can be used)

Heat oil and brown meat. Reduce heat, add onions and garlic and cook until brown. Add tomato sauce, carrots, zucchini and water. Simmer 1 1/2 hours. Add peas and simmer another 30 minutes. Serve over kibble or on a bed of rice.

This can be frozen in single-serving portions.

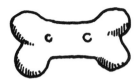

Vegetable Loaf

A LOAF WITH SOME REAL SPRING

Serves 6

1   tablespoon olive oil

1   clove garlic, chopped

1   medium yellow onion, chopped

1   large tomato, chopped

6   cups cooked brown rice

1   teaspoon oregano

1/4   cup chopped fresh parsley

2   eggs, beaten

1   cup grated carrots

1/2   cup grated zucchini

1   cup low-salt chicken broth

Preheat oven to 350 degrees.

Heat oil in a frying pan. Sauté garlic, onion and tomato for 5 minutes. Combine with the remaining ingredients in a large bowl and mix well. In a lightly greased loaf pan, spoon in mixture. Bake for 50 minutes, cool and serve.

May Day . . .
May Day . . .

A Spring Celebration

Spring is finally here, and the celebration of May Day is typi-
fied by a light fare served on linen cloths beneath the shade
of an old oak tree. As the meal is laid out, Webster's curios-
ity draws him to the colorful flowers which lend their fra-
grance to our picnic. Of course, he is quickly drawn back to
our picnic by the fragrances of delicious food!

Turkey Cutlets

Serves 4

4 boneless turkey breasts, skinned and pounded
   very thin

2 eggs, beaten

1 1/2 cups seasoned bread crumbs mixed with
   2 tablespoons wheat germ

4 tablespoons olive oil

Dip turkey in eggs. Roll in bread crumbs. Heat oil and sauté
turkey until brown on both sides and cooked through. Slice
in strips and serve.

Tuna Delight with a Broccoli Bite

Serves 4

1 1/2 cups cooked elbow macaroni

1 cup lowfat milk

1 cup grated cheddar cheese

1 cup chopped fresh broccoli

8 ounces canned tuna, drained

1 tablespoon chopped onion

1/4 cup seasoned bread crumbs mixed with
2 tablespoons wheat germ

Preheat oven to 350 degrees.

Combine all ingredients except bread-crumb mixture and mix well. Spoon into a lightly greased casserole dish. Sprinkle with bread-crumb mixture. Bake for 30 minutes. Cool and serve.

Spinach Rice

Serves 6

1   package frozen chopped spinach

1/2 cup chopped onion

1   clove garlic, chopped

1   tablespoon olive oil

1/2 cup chopped carrots

1/2 teaspoon thyme leaves

2   cups cooked brown rice

1   cup nonfat cottage cheese

Preheat oven to 350 degrees.

Defrost spinach. Sauté garlic and onions in oil until soft (approximately 5 minutes). Mix with remaining ingredients and spoon into a lightly greased baking dish. Bake for 25 to 30 minutes.

The Wedding

Wedding Bells

For a truly important occasion, a little culinary creativity is just the way to make the day really special. And the wedding is always such a big event. When the day finally arrives to take those special vows, a feast will be in order!

The Main Event—Brisket for 20

Did You Say Brisket Dinner?

Serves 20

- 3 tablespoons vegetable oil
- 1 small brisket of beef
- 1 tablespoon salt and pepper, mixed together
- 2 onions, thinly sliced
- 1 cup low-salt tomato sauce
- 2 cups low-salt beef broth

In a Dutch oven, heat oil. Season meat with salt and pepper and sear on both sides. Lower heat, add onions, tomato sauce and beef broth. Cover tightly and simmer for about 2 1/2 to 3 hours until the meat is tender. Cool and serve.

This can be stored in single-serving portions and frozen.

Brown Rice Fit to Be Fed

Serves 4

2 cups low-salt beef broth

1 cup instant brown rice

1 large onion, chopped

1 tablespoon chopped garlic

In a medium saucepan, bring beef broth to a boil. Add remaining ingredients. Cover and simmer for 20 minutes. Recipe may be doubled.

FIDO

Brown rice is wonderful mixed with kibble.

Cookies

MAX'S MID-MEAL MUNCH

Makes 4–5 dozen

2   cups whole-wheat flour

2/3   cup yellow cornmeal

1/2   cup shelled sunflower seeds

2   tablespoons corn oil

1/2   cup low-salt beef broth

2   eggs mixed with 1/4 cup lowfat milk

Glaze

Beat 1 egg. Lightly brush on cookie before baking.

Preheat oven to 350 degrees.

In a large bowl, mix dry ingredients and seeds together. Add oil, broth and egg mixture. Your dough should be firm. Let sit 15 to 20 minutes. On a lightly floured surface, roll out dough 1/4-inch thick. Cut into shapes and brush with glaze. Bake for 25 to 35 minutes until golden brown. Cool. Store cookies in an airtight container.

This dough can also used for Triple Decker Delight (see page 38).

FIDO

Between meals, healthy snacks are okay in moderation.

Triple Decker Delight

A Jewel of a Wedding Cake

This recipes makes two—one for the bride and one for the groom!

The Wedding Cake is a three-step process. If you are going to bake and assemble the cake the same day, allow approximately three hours. If you don't want to prepare it all at once, you can make the cookies, liver filling and frosting a day or two ahead. Keep the cookies in an airtight container, and refrigerate the liver filling and frosting.

Cake Base

Use Max's Mid-Meal Munch cookie recipe (page 37). Roll out the dough and cut six 3-inch round circles, 1/4-inch thick. Bake at 350 degrees for 25 to 35 minutes until golden brown.

Liver Filling

2 tablespoons butter	1 small onion, chopped
1/2 pound liver	1 hard-boiled egg

Melt butter in a medium fry pan. Sauté liver and onions over medium heat for 10 to 15 minutes. Drain and cool. Chop liver-and-onion mixture in a food processor or blender until a thick paste is formed.

Chop the egg and set aside.

Frosting

1 cup nonfat cottage cheese

In a blender or food processor, mix until smooth.

Assembly

Spread a medium layer of the liver mixture on top of a cookie. Lightly sprinkle chopped egg. Place another cookie on top and repeat process. Place the third and final cookie on top and frost the cake with the cottage cheese frosting. Serve the cake whole.

Specialties
with Sparkle

Independence Day Picnic

Lay out a blanket, put up an umbrella and pull out a Frisbee. For our family, Fourth of July has always been a day to party, swim and eat to our content. When everyone is fully satiated, pick a spot on the blanket and enjoy an evening sky full of sparkles.

"Pasta-Bilities"

Your pooch will love these.

Serves 4

4–6 pounds spaghetti squash

1/4 cup olive oil

2 cloves fresh garlic, minced or pressed

2–3 plum tomatoes, chopped and seeded

1 medium zucchini, chopped

1/2 pound fresh mushrooms, sliced

1/4 cup fresh cilantro leaves (optional)

Preheat oven to 400 degrees.

Cut squash lengthwise (discard seeds) and place cut side down in a baking dish one quarter full of water. Bake for 45 minutes until tender. Let cool.

Heat half the olive oil with garlic in a sauté pan. Sauté tomatoes and zucchini for 3 to 4 minutes on medium-high heat. Add mushrooms and cook 1 minute. For added zest, finish with chopped cilantro.

Using a fork, scrape out the center of the squash—the strands will look just like spaghetti—and sauté for 1 minute in remaining olive oil. Top with sauce and serve.

FIDO

Kelly really surprised us with this one. Webster and Max spent all of thirty seconds looking and sniffing before digging in.

Star-Spangled Meat Loaf

Serves 4

1 pound ground beef

2 tablespoons rolled oats

1/2 cup cooked brown rice

3 tablespoons chopped onion

3 tablespoons chopped garlic

2 tablespoons chopped fresh parsley

1 tablespoon ketchup

1 egg, beaten

1 teaspoon Worcestershire sauce

3 hard-boiled eggs

Preheat oven to 350 degrees.

Mix all ingredients well, reserving the boiled eggs. Place mixture in a loaf pan. Make a small valley in the loaf and place the hard-boiled eggs in the center. Cover the eggs with the meat. (Don't forget to take the shells off the eggs!) Bake for 1 hour or until thoroughly cooked.

Pupsicles for a Hot Day

This recipe is quick, easy and fun. It's probably best to serve these treats outside to avoid water on your carpet.

2/3 cup water

2 cups low-salt beef or chicken broth

2-3 ice cube trays

Mix water with the beef or chicken broth. Pour into ice trays. Place in freezer and serve cold. For an extra treat, add a rawhide stick halfway through freezing. Serve outside.

FIDO

Dogs love to chew on ice cubes. Ice cubes are good during summer months, as they keep the drinking water cool and the pup hydrated. While traveling, ice cubes can replace water in your pet's carrier water dish. This will help to prevent spillage.

A tip for puppy owners: Rubbing ice cubes on your pup's gums can help relieve the pains associated with new teeth and diminish teething tendencies. Wrapping the ice cube in a clean rag provides your little one with a helpful fun toy.

The Birthday Bonanza

Max's Favorite

"I'm the birthday boy. It's my birthday week. I'm having a big party with lots of presents and cake because I'm the birthday boy and you have to be nice to me!"

Sloppy Joe Dinner

A MEAL MEANT TO BE MESSY

Serves 4

 1 pound ground beef

1/2 cup chopped onion

 1 tablespoon chopped garlic

1/2 cup chopped carrots

 1 cup low-salt beef broth

Mix all ingredients together and place in a frying pan. Cook over medium heat until meat is cooked through. Drain most of the fat and add the beef broth. Simmer for 10 minutes. If you desire more gravy, add more beef broth.

FROM KELLY ANN'S KITCHEN

Chilly Chicken Rice Supreme

A SALAD FOR ALL SEASONS!

Serves 4

1 1/2 cups cold cooked brown rice

1/2 cup diced cooked chicken

1/2 cup diced cooked carrots

1/4 cup chopped scallions

1/4 cup chopped fresh parsley

1 tablespoon olive oil

In a large bowl, mix all ingredients and toss with the olive oil. This is perfect for that birthday picnic!

FIDO

On those hot summer days when appetites are at a low, this dish will perk them up. Chicken rice is a favorite dish of Webster's. He always comes back for more.

Bethann's Carrot Rice

Serves 6

2 cups cooked brown rice

2 cups grated carrots

1 cup cooked chunked chicken

1 cup grated Swiss cheese

1 large yellow onion, chopped

1 egg, beaten

1/4 cup low-salt chicken broth

1/4 cup vegetable oil

1/4 cup chopped fresh parsley

Preheat oven to 350 degrees.

Mix all ingredients. Spoon into lightly greased casserole dish and bake for 50 minutes to 1 hour. Cool and serve.

Cookies with Chicken Broth

MAX'S MIDNIGHT SNACK

Makes 48–60 cookies

2 cups whole-wheat flour

2/3 cup yellow cornmeal

1/2 cup shelled sunflower seeds

2 tablespoons corn oil

1/2 cup chicken broth

2 eggs mixed with 1/4 cup lowfat milk

Glaze

Beat 1 egg. Lightly brush on cookie before baking.

Preheat oven to 350 degrees.

In a large bowl, mix dry ingredients and sunflower seeds together. Add oil, broth and egg mixture. Your dough should be firm. Let sit 15 to 20 minutes. On a lightly floured surface, roll out dough 1/4-inch thick. Cut into shapes and brush with glaze. Bake for 25 to 35 minutes until golden brown. Cool. Store cookies in an airtight container.

The Hunt Lunch (Without the Fox)

An Autumn Meal

September means a nip in the air and a collage of fall foliage. Although the boys have never been on a hunt, you can bet your right paw they would never miss the Hunt Lunch or an opportunity to spend a day at the stables.

Egg Drop Soup

Serves 6

- 4 cups low-salt chicken broth
- 1/2 cup chopped carrots
- 1/2 cup chopped celery
- 1 tablespoon low-salt soy sauce
- 2 eggs, beaten

Bring the chicken broth to a boil. Add chopped carrots, celery and soy sauce. Simmer for 15 to 20 minutes. Bring soup back to a boil and slowly add beaten eggs with one hand while the other hand is stirring the soup. Let egg cook for 5 minutes. The egg will look like string. Cool and serve with kibble croutons.

Chicken Kabobs

Serves 6

1/2 cup vegetable oil

1/4 cup low-salt soy sauce

1/4 teaspoon garlic powder

1/4 teaspoon chopped onion

1/4 cup orange juice

  4 chicken breasts, cut into 2-inch pieces

  1 medium onion, quartered

  2 large zucchini, cut into large pieces

Combine first five ingredients with the chicken pieces and marinate for 2 hours in the refrigerator. Remove chicken from marinade and alternately place chicken, onion and zucchini on skewers. Brush with leftover marinade. Place on grill and cook for 20 minutes. Remove from skewers. Cool and serve.

Paula T.'s Rice

Serves 4

1 tablespoon butter or margarine

1/2 cup chopped onion

1 cup long grain white rice

2 cups low-salt chicken broth

1/2 cup chopped fresh parsley

In a saucepan, melt butter or margarine and sauté onion until soft. Add rice and mix. Add chicken broth and parsley. Bring to a boil. Cover and simmer for 20 minutes. Remove from heat and let sit covered for an additional 5 minutes. Cool and serve. Good served with Egg Drop Soup (see page 57).

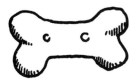

Peanut-Oat Cookies

Directly from the peanut gallery. Guaranteed not to stick to the roof of your mouth!

Makes 24 cookies

1/2 cup butter or margarine, softened

1/2 cup brown sugar

1 egg, beaten

1/4 cup smooth peanut butter

1 cup whole-wheat flour

1/2 teaspoon baking soda

1 cup rolled oats

2 tablespoons wheat germ

Preheat oven to 350 degrees.

Cream together butter and sugar. Add egg and beat well. Stir in peanut butter until smooth. Mix flour and baking soda; then add to mixture. Mix in oats and wheat germ until well blended.

Drop by spoonfuls onto greased cookie sheet and flatten with a fork to make a design. Bake for 12 to 14 minutes.

FIDO

These cookies are rich and should only be given one or two at a time on very special occasions.

Ghosts, Goblins and Doggie Delights

Halloween Night

Trick or Treat. . . . Trick or Treat. . . . The boys like to see how many sweets they can eat. I have created the costume party, complete with healthy Halloween fare, as a nutritious alternative to trick-or-treating. Max is the first in his costume and the last to leave the table.

Fried Rice

Serves 6

3 tablespoons vegetable oil

1/2 cup chopped onion

1/2 cup cooked chunked carrots

1/2 cup cooked peas

1/2 cup chunked ham

2 cups cold cooked brown rice

1 tablespoon low-salt soy sauce

In a large skillet, heat oil. Add onion and carrots. Sauté until onions are translucent. Add peas, ham, rice and soy sauce. Cook for 10 minutes over medium heat while stirring.

Low-Cal Grilled Vegetables
for the Barbecue

Serves 4

olive oil

3 purple onions, peeled and cut in half

1 large eggplant, cut into 1-inch-thick rounds

2 zucchini, halved lengthwise

2 yellow squash, halved lengthwise

1 large red pepper, halved and seeded

1 large yellow pepper, halved and seeded

6 large scallions, both ends trimmed

Baste all veggies with olive oil on both sides (I use a pastry brush). Start with the onions, cook 2 minutes and then add eggplant, zucchini and squash. Let grill 3 to 4 minutes, occasionally basting with the olive oil. As vegetables are done cooking, set aside in a bowl and allow natural juices to surface. When all vegetables are cooked, cut into bite-sized pieces.

FIDO

You'll be surprised at just how much dogs enjoy tastily prepared vegetables. True, most would no sooner chomp on a head of lettuce than you or I, but add a little creativity to your mix, and you might be surprised.

Open Sesame Chicken

Serves 4

1 cup toasted sesame seeds

1 teaspoon thyme*

1 teaspoon sweet basil*

1 teaspoon rosemary*

2 eggs, lightly beaten

1/3 cup all-purpose flour

1/2 teaspoon black pepper

1/2 teaspoon salt

4 boneless chicken breasts, skinned and pounded 1/4-inch thick

2 tablespoons olive oil

*preferrably dry herbs

Preheat oven to 350 degrees.

In the first bowl, combine sesame seeds and herbs. In a second bowl, beat eggs. In a third bowl, mix flour, pepper and salt. Dredge chicken breasts into flour, then into eggs, and press into sesame seeds. Brown in olive oil. Bake for 25 minutes. When cool, slice and serve on a bed of kibble.

Black and White Muffins

Makes 12 small muffins

1/4 cup brown sugar

1/4 cup light molasses

1/2 cup corn oil

1 cup lowfat milk

1 teaspoon vanilla

2 cups all-purpose flour

1 tablespoon baking powder

1/2 teaspoon baking soda

1/2 cup carob chips (available at a health-food store)

Preheat oven to 400 degrees.

In a large bowl combine brown sugar, molasses, corn oil, milk and vanilla. Mix well. Then add all the dry ingredients. Mix well. Slowly fold in the carob chips. Spoon mixture into muffin tins and bake for 20 minutes. Cool. These can be frozen.

FIDO

Remember to always use carob instead of chocolate. Chocolate can be very dangerous for your pet.

Let's Talk Turkey

A Thanksgiving Feast

In our house, Thanksgiving is the biggest party of the year. The Manhattan Turkey has become a tradition for man, woman and dog alike. When we all sit down to Thanksgiving dinner, the house is bursting with hungry guests, and no one feels left out of the festivities.

Zucchini Pancakes

Serves 4

3 cups coarsely grated and peeled zucchini

1 egg

1/2 cup flour

1 teaspoon baking powder

In a large bowl, combine zucchini and egg. Add flour and baking powder. Mix well. Drop by the spoonful on a hot skillet with a little oil or butter. Cook until light brown on both sides.

Bird in a Pan

TURKEY LOAF WITH STUFFING

Serves 2

1 pound ground turkey	1 1/2 tablespoons chopped garlic
1 egg, beaten	3 tablespoons chopped onion
1 cup cooked brown rice	
1/2 cup chopped celery	1 cup low-salt chicken broth
1/2 cup chopped carrots	
1/2 cup chopped fresh parsley	1 cup of your favorite stuffing

Preheat oven to 350 degrees.

In a large bowl, mix turkey, egg, rice, celery, carrots, parsley, garlic and onion. Blend well. In a medium bowl, blend chicken broth and stuffing. Add to the turkey mixture. Shape into a loaf pan and bake for 1 1/2 hours or until done.

This has no bones, and generally no leftovers.

72

Chicken Loaf

MORE CLUCK FOR YOUR BUCK

Serves 2

- 1 pound ground chicken
- 1 cup cooked brown rice
- 1 egg, beaten
- 1/4 cup chopped fresh parsley
- 2 tablespoons minced fresh garlic
- 3 tablespoons wheat germ
- 1/2 cup chopped carrots

Preheat oven to 350 degrees.

In a large bowl, mix all ingredients. Form into a loaf pan and bake for 1 hour or until done. Cool and serve. Slice Chicken Loaf and serve over kibble.

> **FIDO**
>
> **If the Colonel ever opens a restaurant serving canine fare, Chicken Loaf would be the most popular entrée.**

Mushroom and Cheese Rice

Serves 6

1 6-oz. package cream cheese

2 eggs

1 can (10 oz.) evaporated milk

1 cup shredded Jarlsberg cheese

1 1/2 pounds sliced fresh mushrooms

4 scallions, both ends removed

2 tablespoons unsalted butter

3 cups cooked rice (preferably brown)

Preheat oven to 350 degrees.

Blend cream cheese, eggs, evaporated milk and cheese. Sauté mushrooms and scallions in butter until brown and drain off juices. Mix rice, mushrooms and cheese mixture together. Put in buttered baking dish and bake for 1 hour covered. Serve with plenty of fresh water.

The Yuletide Dog

Christmas Dinner

Dashing through the snow on a one horse open sleigh; across the fields we go, barking all the way . . . woof, woof, woof!

Chicken Pot Pie without the Crust

Serves 4

1   whole chicken, deboned and cut into bite-size pieces

1   small onion, chopped

2   tablespoons butter or margarine

3   tablespoons flour

2   cups low-salt chicken broth

1   bay leaf

1 1/4   teaspoons dried tarragon leaves

Brown chicken pieces with onions in butter in a Dutch oven or large saucepan. Blend flour with 1/4 cup broth. Add this mixture to chicken with the bay leaf and remaining chicken broth. Cover and simmer for 30 minutes. Add tarragon and cook for 5 more minutes. Remove bay leaf and serve at room temperature. Leftovers can be frozen for your next dinner.

Veggie Pudding

Serves 4

3 cups chopped carrots

2 cups low-salt chicken broth

1/2 cup lowfat milk

1 cup cooked brown rice

2 tablespoons wheat germ

1 1/2 cups frozen peas, defrosted

Preheat oven to 350 degrees.

Cook carrots in chicken broth until tender. Drain and save 1 cup of liquid. In a food processor or blender, blend carrots, milk and the saved chicken broth until smooth. Add brown rice, wheat germ and peas. Spoon into lightly greased baking dish. Bake uncovered for 30 minutes.

St. Nick's Snack

Makes 3–4 dozen

3	cups whole-wheat flour
1	cup yellow cornmeal
1	cup rolled oats
2/3	cup nonfat dry milk
2	tablespoons garlic powder
1 1/2	cups low-salt chicken broth
1/2	cup corn oil
2	eggs

Glaze

Beat 1 egg. Lightly brush on cookie before baking.

Preheat oven to 350 degrees.

Mix the flour, cornmeal, oatmeal, dry milk and garlic powder in a large bowl. Form a well in the middle of the mixture. Whisk chicken broth, corn oil and 2 eggs in another bowl. Stir this into flour mixture and blend until a stiff dough forms. An extra 1/4 to 1/2 cup of whole-wheat flour can be added if the dough is not stiff enough. Let dough rest for 20 to 25 minutes. Roll out dough on a floured surface; try to keep it as thin as possible. Cut dough into shapes with your favorite cookie cutter. Brush with glaze. Bake for 25 to 30 minutes. Store cookies in an airtight container.

FIDO

If you do not have the time to roll the dough out flat, roll it into a log shape, chill, then slice and bake.

Pea Soup

Anderson's eat your heart out!

Serves 4

2 1/2 cups low-salt chicken broth

   2 large potatoes, peeled and chunked

   2 cups frozen peas

   1 cup cooked chicken, chunked

In a small broth pot (or large saucepan) place chicken broth and potatoes. Boil for 25 to 30 minutes or until potatoes are tender. Add peas and cook an additional 5 minutes. Cool for 20 minutes. In a blender or food processor, blend mixture until smooth. Add chicken pieces and serve cold.

Barkmitzvah

At a Year and Three Quarters

"Boys, you are no longer pups. The time has come for you to be dogs!"

Chicken Liver Pâté

A Tradition!

Serves 4

   2   tablespoons butter or margarine

1/2   pound chicken livers

   1   small onion, chopped

   2   hard-boiled eggs

Heat butter or margarine in a frying pan. Sauté chicken livers and onions over medium heat, stirring occasionally, for approximately 10 to 15 minutes until cooked through. Chop liver, onions and eggs in a food processor or blender, a little at a time. Mold into shape and refrigerate for several hours. Serve with Garlic Snaps (see page 88 for recipe).

Chicken Soup with Matzo Balls

MAX'S MOTHER'S TOUCH

Serves 6

4 quarts cold water

4 pounds chicken necks, backs and legs

4 carrots, chopped

3 stalks of celery with leaves

2 onions, chopped

1 leek, chopped

1 cup chopped fresh parsley

2 bay leaves

Place all ingredients in an 8- to 10-quart soup pot. Cover with cold water and bring to a boil. Reduce heat and simmer for 2 1/2 hours partially covered. When cool, strain through a colander with some cheesecloth to catch all the bones and vegetables. Place soup in container, let cool and refrigerate overnight. The next day, the fat will have hardened on top—simply remove. Save 1/2 cup fat for the matzo balls. Soup can be frozen.

FIDO

This soup can be used as chicken stock for other recipes. For the extra special touch, add cooked boneless chicken.

Matzo Balls

6 eggs

1 tablespoon finely chopped parsley

1 tablespoon finely chopped onion

1/2 cup chicken fat from the top of the soup

2/3 cup hot water

1 1/2 cups matzo meal

Beat eggs lightly. Add parsley, onion, chicken fat and water. Slowly add matzo meal. Mix well and refrigerate for 2 hours. Drop the mixture by the spoonful into rapidly boiling soup (see page 84). Reduce heat and cook slowly for 1 hour, uncovered. Serve at room temperature.

FIDO

Remember your four-legged guests require room temperature food.

Liver and Onion Crisps

Makes 6–8 dozen crackers

1 pound cooked chicken livers, boiled (See "Before You Begin" for preparation instructions page xvii)

1 medium-size onion, chopped

1 cup low-salt beef broth

1 1/2 cups wheat germ

2 tablespoons brewer's yeast (optional)

1 cup yellow cornmeal

2 cups whole-wheat flour

onion powder

Glaze

Beat 1 egg. Lightly brush on cookie before baking.

Preheat oven to 350 degrees.

Using a blender or food processor, purée the liver and onion while slowly adding beef broth. When all the liver is puréed, transfer to a large bowl. Blend in wheat germ and brewer's yeast. Slowly add cornmeal and whole-wheat flour until the dough becomes stiff. Knead dough for 3 to 5 minutes and let it rest for an additional 5 minutes. On a lightly floured surface, roll the dough into a ball.

As Webster and Max like their crackers thin, I have found that the best way to do this is to split the ball into four sections and roll each section into a hot-dog shape. Wrap these in plastic wrap and chill for 30 minutes. Slice into very thin chips. Place the chips on a lightly greased cookie sheet (a light cooking spray is good for this purpose) and brush with glaze. Lightly sprinkle with onion powder and bake for 25 to 40 minutes. Halfway through, turn. As the crackers cool, they will become hard. Leftover dough can be frozen for up to 3 months.

Garlic Snaps

Makes 6–8 dozen

1 pound cooked boneless chicken, white and dark

2 cloves garlic, peeled

1 cup low-salt chicken broth

1 1/2 cups wheat germ

2 tablespoons brewer's yeast (optional)

2 cups whole-wheat flour (more may be needed)

1 cup yellow cornmeal

garlic powder

Glaze

Beat I egg. Lightly brush on cookie before baking.

Preheat oven to 350 degrees.

In a large blender or food processor, gradually purée chicken and garlic, slowly adding chicken broth. Transfer the chicken purée into a large bowl. Mix in wheat germ and brewer's yeast. Slowly add flour and cornmeal until the dough becomes stiff. Knead the dough for 3 to 5 minutes, then let it rest for 5 to 10 minutes. On a lightly floured surface, roll the dough into a ball.

See the Liver and Onion Crisps recipe (page 86) to make thin crackers. Place the chips on a lightly greased cookie sheet (a light cooking spray is good for this purpose) and brush with glaze. Lightly sprinkle with garlic powder and bake for 25 to 40 minutes. Halfway through, turn. As the crackers cool, they will become hard. Leftover dough can be frozen for up to 3 months.

FIDO

This is a real crowd pleaser. Most guests enjoy the flavor of garlic . . . except for the fleas.

The Saucy Dog

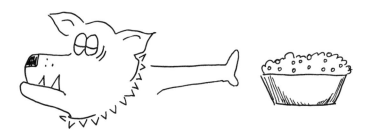

Tantalizing Toppings

In this section, you'll find edible suggestions to help you win the waiting game. You know . . . when you and your pet are nose-to-nose, seeing who will give in first. Will a new brand of dog food be bought, or will your pup give in and eat kibble?

To turn the table in this test of wills, I often add a gravy or sauce to the kibble, mixing well so they don't just eat the sauce. Adding small amounts to their regular kibble gives extra flavor without altering their diet.

Barbecue Sauce

For that home-on-the-range favor.

1 small green pepper, chopped

1 clove garlic, chopped

1 cup low-salt tomato sauce

1/4 cup Worcestershire sauce

1/4 cup ketchup

1/4 cup brown sugar

1/4 cup red wine vinegar

1 medium onion, chopped

2 cups water

Combine all the ingredients. Simmer for 30 minutes. Cool and serve or store in an airtight container in the refrigerator.

FIDO

This sauce is wonderful with ground beef and good on most other dishes as well.

Chicken or Beef Broth Gravy

2 tablespoons cornstarch

2 cups low-salt chicken or beef broth

In a saucepan, add the cornstarch to the broth and bring to a boil. Thicken. Serve at room temperature. For a change, add small amounts of leftover chicken, turkey, beef or vegetables.

Turkey Gravy

2 tablespoons all-purpose flour

2 tablespoons drippings from a roasted turkey

2 cups boiling water

1/2 cup cooked chopped giblets (optional)

Over medium heat, blend flour and drippings to create a rue (thick paste). Slowly add boiling water while whisking until gravy thickens. Add giblets.

The Whooped Pooch

Remedies for What Ails You

You'll notice that throughout this book, I have included numerous rice recipes. I have done this not only because Webster and Max love rice, but because cooked rice is especially good for firming the stool. Remember to always check with your veterinarian when you notice anything unusual regarding your dog's health. Moderation should be your guide. Too much rice can cause constipation, and you'll find yourself with a new set of problems.

Plain Boiled Rice

Serves 4

2 cups water

1 cup long grain white rice

In a saucepan, bring water to a boil. Add rice and stir. Turn temperature down and cover rice. Simmer for 20 minutes. Remove from heat and keep covered for an additional 5 minutes. Cool, and serve plain or with Boiled Burger (see page 96).

Boiled Burger

Serves 2

6–8 cups water

1 pound ground beef

In a large saucepan or small soup pot, bring water to a boil. Add meat, breaking it up as you add to water. Boil for 15 to 20 minutes until cooked through. Drain in a colander and rinse well. Cool and serve with Plain Boiled Rice (see page 95).

FIDO

Of course your dog doesn't like to take his medicine, but administering medication doesn't have to be a real pill. Here's a trick we use at our house. I bury the pill in a treat and begin praising Webster like I normally would before giving him something special. Then I pop the treat in his mouth and we're done. The best camouflage material is a piece of cheese, soft white bread rolled into a small ball or his favorite—chunky peanut butter. Be sure to confirm with your veterinarian that the pill can be given with food.

Add Your Own Recipes

Send Us Your Recipes

Please send us your suggestions for healthy recipes.

If there is a lipsmacking response, we will include these—with your permission—in our next book.

Conversion
Tables

Liquid Measures

American Cup	Imperial Cup
1/4 cup	4 tablespoons
1/3 cup	5 tablespoons
1/2 cup	8 tablespoons
2/3 cup	1/4 pint
3/4 cup	1/4 pint + 2 tablespoons
1 cup	1/4 pint + 6 tablespoons
1 1/4 cups	1/2 pint
1 1/2 cups	1/2 pint + 4 tablespoons
2 cups	3/4 pint
2 1/2 cups	1 pint
3 cups	1 1/2 pints
4 cups	1 1/2 pints + 4 tablespoons
5 cups	2 pints

Solid Measures

American Cup	Imperial Cup
Butter	
1 tablespoon	1/2 ounce
1/4 cup	2 ounces
1/2 cup	4 ounces
1 cup	8 ounces
Cheese (grated)	
1/2 cup	2 ounces
Cornmeal	
1 cup	6 ounces
Flour	
1/4 cup	1 1/4 ounces
1/2 cup	2 1/2 ounces
1 cup	5 ounces
1 1/2 cups	7 1/2 ounces
2 cups	10 ounces
Herbs	
1/4 cup	1/4 ounce
Sugar	
1/4 cup	1 3/4 ounces

American Cup	Imperial Cup
1/2 cup	3 ounces
1 cup	6 1/2 ounces
Vegetables	
1/2 cup	2 ounces
1 cup	4 ounces
Wheat Germ	
1/2 cup	1 1/2 ounces
1 cup	3 ounces

Oven Temperatures

	°F	Gas Mark	°C
Cool	225–250	1/4–1/2	110–120
Very Slow	250–275	1/2–1	120–140
Slow	275–300	1–2	140–150
Very Moderate	300–350	2–3	150–160
Moderate	375	4	180
Moderately Hot	400	5–6	190–200
Hot	425–450	7–8	220–230
Very Hot	450–475	8–9	230–240

Ingredient Names

All-purpose flour = Plain flour

Brown sugar = Soft brown sugar

Baking soda = Bicarbonate of soda

Molasses = Treacle

INDEX